28

Story & Art by Yoshiki Nakamura

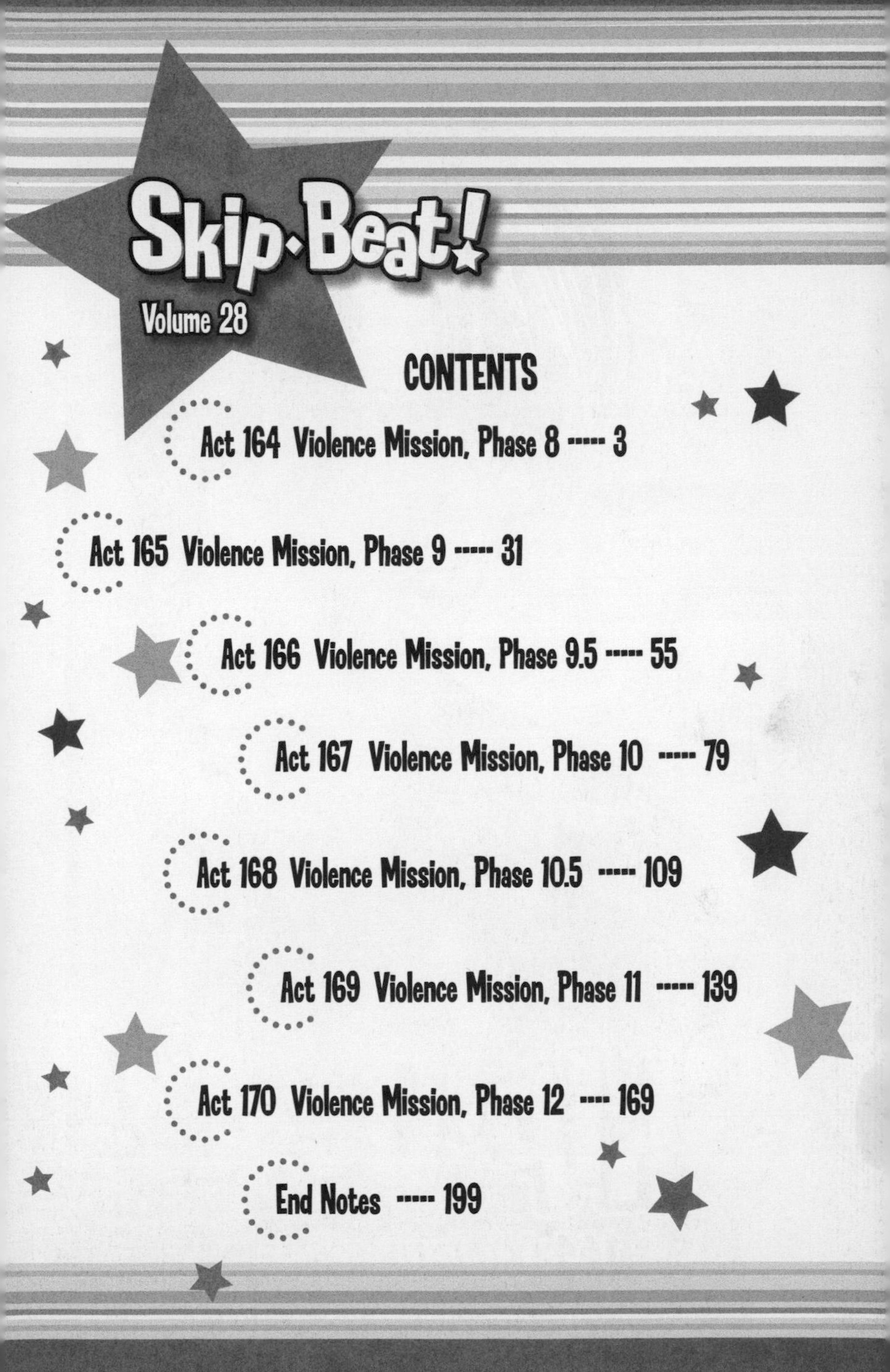

Skip·Beat!

Volume 28

CONTENTS

Skip·Beat!
Act 164: Violence Mission, Phase 8

IT CAME OFF...
ARE YOU OKAY?
UH ...
HUH ?
YES!

THE CHAIN SOMETIMES POPS OPEN CUZ...
...IT'S A CHEAP ONE I BOUGHT AT YOROZUYA.
OH.
GOOD...
...THEN YOU DON'T NEED TO WORRY.
HUH?
THERE'S THIS OLD SAYING...
...THAT WHEN A CHAIN BREAKS...
...IT'S AN OMEN THAT SOMETHING UNLUCKY IS GONNA HAPPEN.
NO.

THAT'S NOT POOOOS-SIBLE.
Unlucky? Noooo.
Heh heh heh heh
THE CHAIN DIDN'T BREAK.
THE CLASP IS JUST LOOSE.
HUH?
WHAT? A CHAIN BROKE?
IT FELL OFF!
How can the CLASP snap?!
THE CLASP IS LOOSE!
Just a bit!
Huh?
WHAT'S THAT?
YOUR CLASP SNAPPED?
On your neck-lace?
IT FELL OFF!
How can the CLASP snap?!
IT FELL OFF!
Just a bit!
THE CLASP SLIPPED OPEN!
IT'S LOOOOOOOOOSE!
RRMMBL
...
Noooo!
All right all right. Don't get any closer!
Please don't curse meee!
You're scaring meeeee!

SHE'S AWFULLY WORKED UP...
For someone who says it isn't unlucky.
IS SHE WORRIED SOMETHING'S REALLY GONNA HAPPEN IF THE CHAIN BREAKS?
...
DUNNO...
AH...
...SHE'S WORRIED ABOUT THEM...
MAYBE...
mrmr
mrmr
mrmr
mrmr

SCREEEEEEE
VROOOOM
BAM
SHK

SCREEEEE

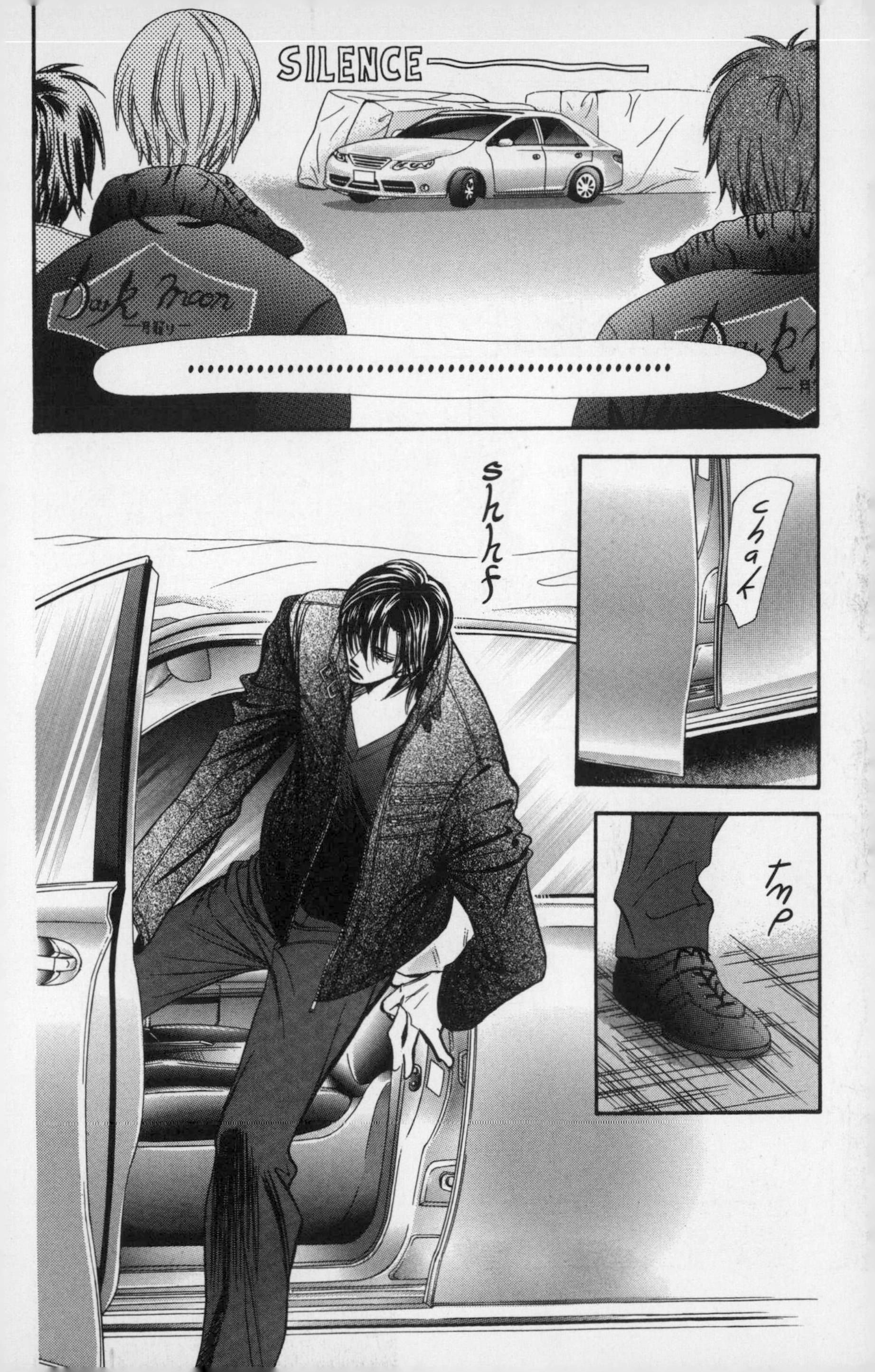
SILENCE
Dark moon
....
chak
shhf
tmp

dazed
...
UMM.
DID I DO SOMETHING WRONG?
Oh!
Wha...
No...
D... DIRECTOR?!
Oh!
N-NO.
THAT WAS GOOD!
UH...
IT WAS WONDERFUL! PERFECT!

DO IT JUST LIKE THAT FOR THE TAPED REHEARSAL!
smile
OKAY.
I'LL GO BACK TO THE START POINT.
UH... ...TSU-RUGA.
YES?
WE'RE ADDING NAOYUKI'S CAR THIS TIME. A STUNTMAN WILL BE DRIVING, SO HE'LL STOP BEFORE THE CARS HIT.
BUT DON'T PUSH YOURSELF.
STOP THE CAR IF SOMETHING DOESN'T FEEL RIGHT.
I WILL.
TSURUGA, WEAR YOUR MOUTH GUARD JUST IN CASE...
Umm
Ah... Okay...
WE'LL FILM IT THIS TIME.
EVERY-ONE PLEEEEASE.
Ye---s!
dash dash
busy busy
...
HOW WAS IT? DID YOU SEE HIM?
HE STOPPED THE CAR AFTER A GORGEOUS SPIN-OUT.

HE WENT AT FULL SPEED, UNLIKE THE TEST DRIVE EARLIER...
I thought he'd blow away the shock absorption wall...
DARN... HE'S SO COOL IT PISSES ME OFF.
IS HE REALLY AN AMATEUR?
No way.
MAYBE HE USED TO BE A PROFES-SIONAL—
A WELL-KNOWN HELL'S ANGEL!
Like Initial ■!
A stuntman is not an option.
BASED ON HOW HE DROVE...
WELL...
...I THINK...
...THEY'LL BE ABLE TO SHOOT A GOOD SCENE SAFELY THAT BOTH REN AND THE DIRECTOR WILL BE HAPPY WITH.
All right, cut!

FRO...
...ZE-I-I-N
AAH...
RUMI, GET UP, GET UP! GET UP NOW!
AAAAARGH.
I...
I'M FREEZE-I-I-ING!
shiver
shake
NO KIDDING.
It's only the end of February.
WAAAAAAH.
RUMI, QUICK. GET INTO THE CAR.
BUT SHE HAS TO HIDE IT FROM THE AUDIENCE...
I sympathize with her a little.
TOO BAD. SHE GOT TOTALLY FROZEN.
Was the take okay?
SINCE THE DRAMA WILL BE BROADCAST IN THE SPRING...

Her mouth guard.
ONE MORE TIME.

KYAAAAAAAAAH!

VROOOOOOOM

ZOOM
NOOOOOO!
WHAM
Peek
HE'S NOT USING HIS BRAKES.
DOOOM
WHOA...
ZOOM

ZOOM
GRAND-MA.
THE LIGHT'S GREEN. CAN WE CROSS NOW?
JUST WAIT.
shhh
WE'LL BE ABLE TO CROSS IN A MOMENT.

AH...
IT'S MOM!
SCREE EEEE
WELL...
NOW'S YOUR TURN, HERO.
VROOOM
SCREEEEEEE
COME AND...

...GET ME!
FWOOSH

WHAT?!

SLAM
SCREEEEEEEEEE
KYAAAAAAAAAH!
?!
WH...
WHAT WAS THAT?!

I HEARD BRAKES SLAMMING...
I HEARD PEOPLE SCREAM...
Even we could hear it.
YOU KNOW ...
DARK MOON IS SHOOTING CLOSE BY...
AND THERE'S THAT CAR CHASE SCENE ...
MAY-BE...
...THERE WAS AN ACCIDENT?

tap
Uh...
Noooo! I can't stop myself!
I've got to go loo—k!
DASH
What?!
D-Direc-toooooor?!
THAT'S NOT FAAAAIR!
Hey!
Don't go off by yourself!
He's simply curious.
Woo!
I...
I WANNA SEE TOOOOO!
He's a dancer, unrestricted and faithful to his desires!
I envy him!
impatient
nervous
fidgeting
Ooh... I'd like to be forced to dance like that...
Wah! Wah!
By her desires
...

WHY DON'T YOU GO TAKE A LOOK?
WHAAT?!
GO SEE WHAT'S GOING ON...
...IF YOU'RE WORRIED.
B...
BUT ...
I'M STILL WORKING...
They were talking about doing shots with only Natsu's group while they wait for Marumi.
THE MAN IN CHARGE WAS THE FIRST ONE TO LEAVE.
I DON'T THINK ANYBODY WILL GET ANGRY AT YOU...

...IF YOU GO SEE WHAT'S GOING ON TOO...
Gah...
YEAH...
YOU JUST NEED TO COME BACK BEFORE THE DIRECTOR.
Ah ha ha
GO ON...
...WE DON'T MIND.

BOW
DASH
IT'S LIKE WHEN SHE ACTED WEIRD AFTER I MENTIONED THE WORD "FAIRY"...
ZOO—M
Wow... she's fast.
SHE ...
...LOOKED REALLY DIFFERENT JUST THEN.
Kyoko.
YEAH.
HER FACE WAS DEATHLY PALE.

OF COURSE SHE'D BE WORRIED ABOUT AN ACCIDENT...
...BUT WOULD SHE LOOK LIKE THAT AFTER CO-STARRING WITH HIM ONCE?
MAYBE KYOKO'S REALLY FRIENDLY...
...WITH HIM?
WHAAT?!
The DARK MOON filming...
The car chase...
Th- The acci- dent...
Mr. Tsuruga is in it?
I...
Kyoko mentioned it.
...THINK SO.
Wha...?
No.
Wha...?!
You seri- ous?!
Um... U...
Um
May I...
May I go take a look too?!
panic panic
fidget fidget
inch inch
worry worry
May I?
You'll let me, right?
I should be able to GO!

I'm GOOOiiiNG!
...
I THOUGHT ...
...SHE SEEMED RESTLESS AFTER WE HEARD DARK MOON WAS SHOOTING NEAR HERE.
SO SHE LIKES HIM...
Ren Tsuruga.
She fooled me...
After we both vowed acting comes first, and men second...
SHE ...
...
...GOT ALL PALE AND TURNED WHITE...
HM ?
OH?
THEN ...
... WHAT?
MAYBE ...

End of Act 164

SCREEEEE
THOOM

Skip·Beat!
Act 165: Violence Mission, Phase 9

DASH
Dark Moon

TSURUGA!
YOU ALL RIGHT ?!
chak
TSU-RUGA ...

ARE YOU HURT?!
TSURUGA?!
MRMR
MRMR
MRMR
MRMR
TSURU...
...GA?

mrmr
mrmr
mrmr
mrmr
WE'RE SORRY...

mrmr
mrmr
mrmr
mrmr
WE'RE REALLY, REALLY SORRY...
Waah! Waah!
I'M JUST GLAD NO ONE WAS HURT.
AH... BUT...

I THINK YOU SHOULD GO TO THE HOSPITAL JUST IN CASE...
NO...
WE DON'T NEED TO...
WE'RE OKAY, REALLY...
mrmr
mrmr

mrmr
mrmr
WE WERE ONLY FRIGHTENED...
FOR A SECOND THERE, I DIDN'T KNOW WHAT WAS GOING TO HAPPEN.
Phew~
I was scared.
I'M GLAD BOTH OF THEM ARE SAFE.
mrmr
mrmr
THAT WAS AMAZING.
THOSE CARS BARELY MISSED THE KID, AND SPUN AROUND HOW MANY TIMES?
Umm
I CAN'T REMEMBER EXACTLY.
THEY DIDN'T STOP AT THE SAME TIME...
...BUT THEY WERE IN SYNC WHILE THEY WERE MOVING.
I CAN'T BELIEVE THEY WERE ABLE TO MAINTAIN THE SAME DISTANCE FROM EACH OTHER WHILE THEY WERE SPINNING.
If their timing was even a second off, they would have crashed into each other.
YOU CAN'T DO THAT UNLESS YOU'RE A REALLY GOOD DRIVER.
Really.
SLAM
Pant

Pant
Pant
Pant
!
glance
AH!

DIREC-TOR OGATA!
HUH?
TH...
THEN ...
THE CARS ONLY SPUN OUT BECAUSE THEY WERE AVOIDING A CHILD?!
YES.
They did spin quite a bit, though.
FORTU-NATELY THE CARS DIDN'T HIT EACH OTHER ...
tmp tmp
...SO I ASSUME TSURUGA ISN'T SERIOUSLY HURT.
I'M SO GLAD ...
...

HMM ...
IS THIS REALLY KYOKO?
SHE'S CHANGED SO MUCH ...
Girls surprise me...
IGA-RASHI.
THANK YOU FOR AVOIDING THAT CHILD AND TSURUGA...
YOU SAVED THE DAY...
bow
YOU'RE NOT HURT?
NO.
I'M ALL RIGHT...
WELL... THAT'S MY JOB.
...BUT TSU-RUGA.
HUH ?!

THERE'S SOMETHING WRONG WITH HIM.
AH.
DIRECTOR.
SOMETHING WRONG?!
HOW'S TSURUGA DOING?!
WELL, UM...
THERE'S SOMETHING REALLY WRONG WITH HIM...
HIS EYES ARE OPEN AND HE'S CONSCIOUS...
...BUT HE'S TOTALLY UNRESPONSIVE.
IT'S LIKE...
...HE CAN'T SEE OR HEAR ANYTHING...

AH...

MR....

...TSURUGA.

HE...

...LOOKS LIKE HE DID...

...THAT TIME...

I LIFTED HIM OFF THE STEERING WHEEL...

...BUT MAYBE I SHOULDN'T HAVE MOVED HIM?!
panic panic
MAYBE HE HIT HIS HEAD?
DON'T KNOW ...
WE NEED TO HAVE A CHECKUP DONE TO SEE...
wave wave
...
TSURUGA?
IT'S LIKE...
...HIS SOUL HAS LEFT HIM.
I'VE OFTEN HEARD THE EXPRESSION "A LIFELESS SHELL"...
...BUT...
...IT'S NOT SIMPLY A METAPHOR RIGHT NOW.

IT'S LIKE...
...HIS SOUL...
...HAS REALLY FLOWN OFF SOME-WHERE...
TSU...
TSU-RUGA!
shiver
...

Aaa~~~h
Aaaah———h!

AHHHHHHHHHHHHHH!
RICK!
NOOO.
PLEASE.
PLEASE...
...RICK.
DON'T DIE!

sway
I GOTTA...
...OR THE BLOOD...
RICK'S...BLOOD...
...WILL ALL...
...FLOW...
...STOP IT...
...OUT...

...
IT'S...
...COLD.
...BEGIN-NING...
I'M...
...TO...
seep
seep

...FREEZE.

I...
...CAN'T MOVE...
End of Act 165

Skip·Beat!
Act 166: Violence Mission, Phase 9.5

OH?
SO YOU'RE HERE TOO.
AH...
THEY LET YOU IN...
...CUZ YOU'RE MIO.
Hey hey, ask them to let me in too.
I'M SORRY FOR COMING OVER HERE WITHOUT PERMISSION ...
A CLOSE CO-STAR GOT INTO AN ACCIDENT, SO IT'S NATURAL YOU'D RUSH OVER HERE.
It's all right.
Since you two belong to the same agency.

I'VE GOT NOTHING TO DO WITH HIM, BUT I RUSHED OVER HERE.
So don't you worry.
OKAY...
He was just curious.
I'M GLAD HE DIDN'T REPRIMAND ME...
...BUT I'M WORRIED...
About him...
SO HOW'S TSURUGA DOING?
UH.
mrmr
mrmr
mrmr
mrmr
UM.
ACTUALLY...
CALL AN AMBULANCE PLEASE.
!
WE'RE CANCELLING THE REST OF TODAY'S FILMING.
...
DIRECTOR...
WHAT'S HAPPENED TO MR. TSURUGA...?
KYOKO.
IT'S NOT GOOD.

HE'S NOT RESPONDING AT ALL.
THERE'S SOMETHING SERIOUSLY WRONG WITH HIM.
I THINK WE SHOULD TAKE HIM TO A HOSPITAL FOR A CHECKUP.
......

MR. ...
... TSU-RUGA?

I WILL NOT FORGIVE YOU.
WHY...
...DID THIS HAVE TO HAPPEN TO RICK?!
IT'S ALL YOUR FAULT!
I'LL NEVER...
...FOR-GIVE YOU...
...EVEN AFTER YOU'RE DEAD.

RICK WOULDN'T HAVE BEEN HURT IF YOU HADN'T BEEN THERE!
IF HE HADN'T BEEN INVOLVED WITH YOU!
IF HE'D NEVER MET YOU...
...RICK WOULDN'T HAVE DIED!
YOU MURDERER...

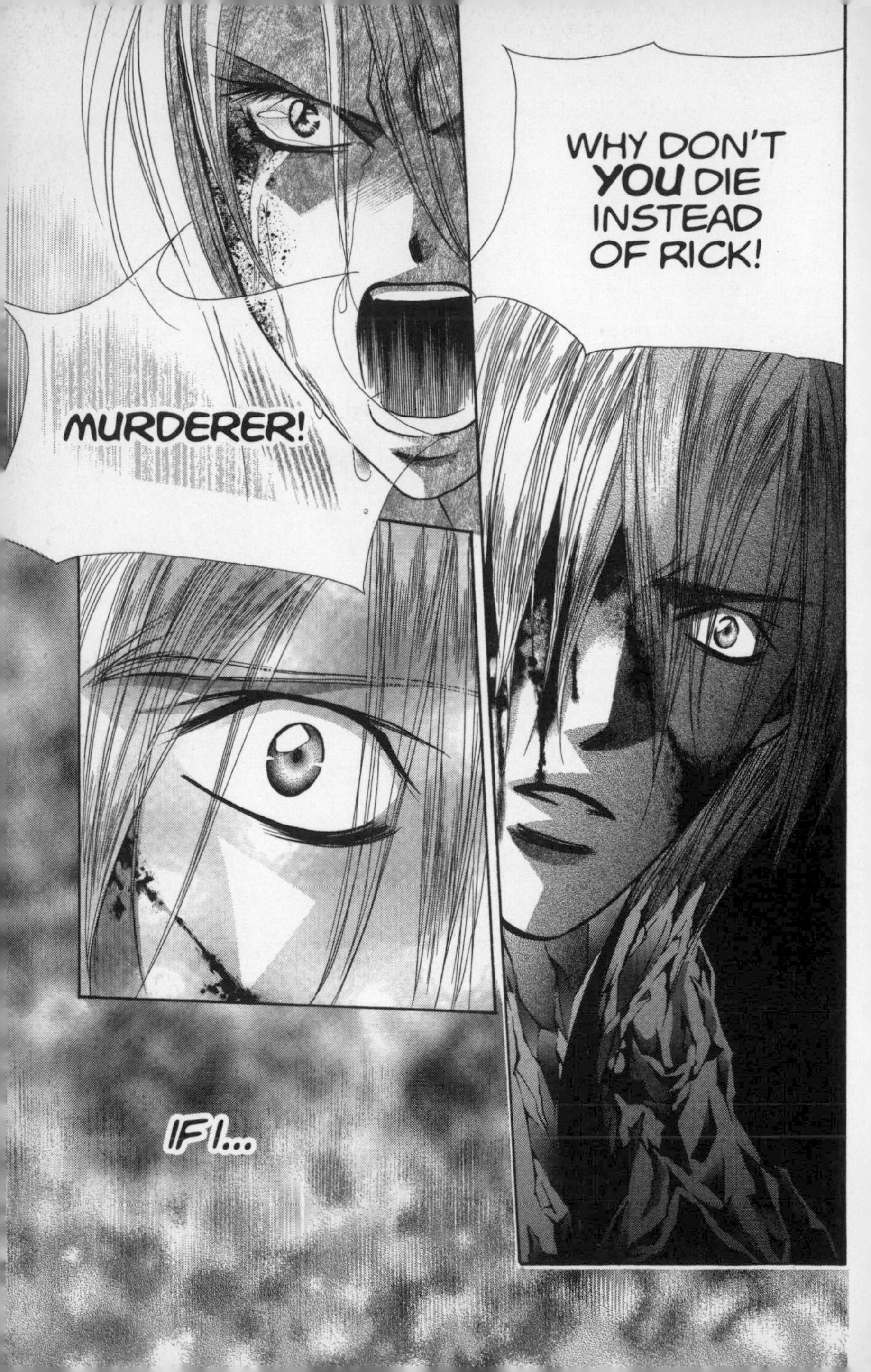
WHY DON'T YOU DIE INSTEAD OF RICK!
MURDERER!
IF I...

...DIE INSTEAD...

...OF RICK...

...WILL RICK...

...BE ALIVE...

...AGAIN?

RICK...

...WANTS...

...IT...

...SO THAT'S...

...WHY...

...MY...

...BODY...

...IS...

...FREEZING?
AH...
OF COURSE.
YES...
YES...

I...
I DON'T...
...MIND.
IF...
...RICK...
...WANTS IT...
THEN.

shgg
...DON'T...

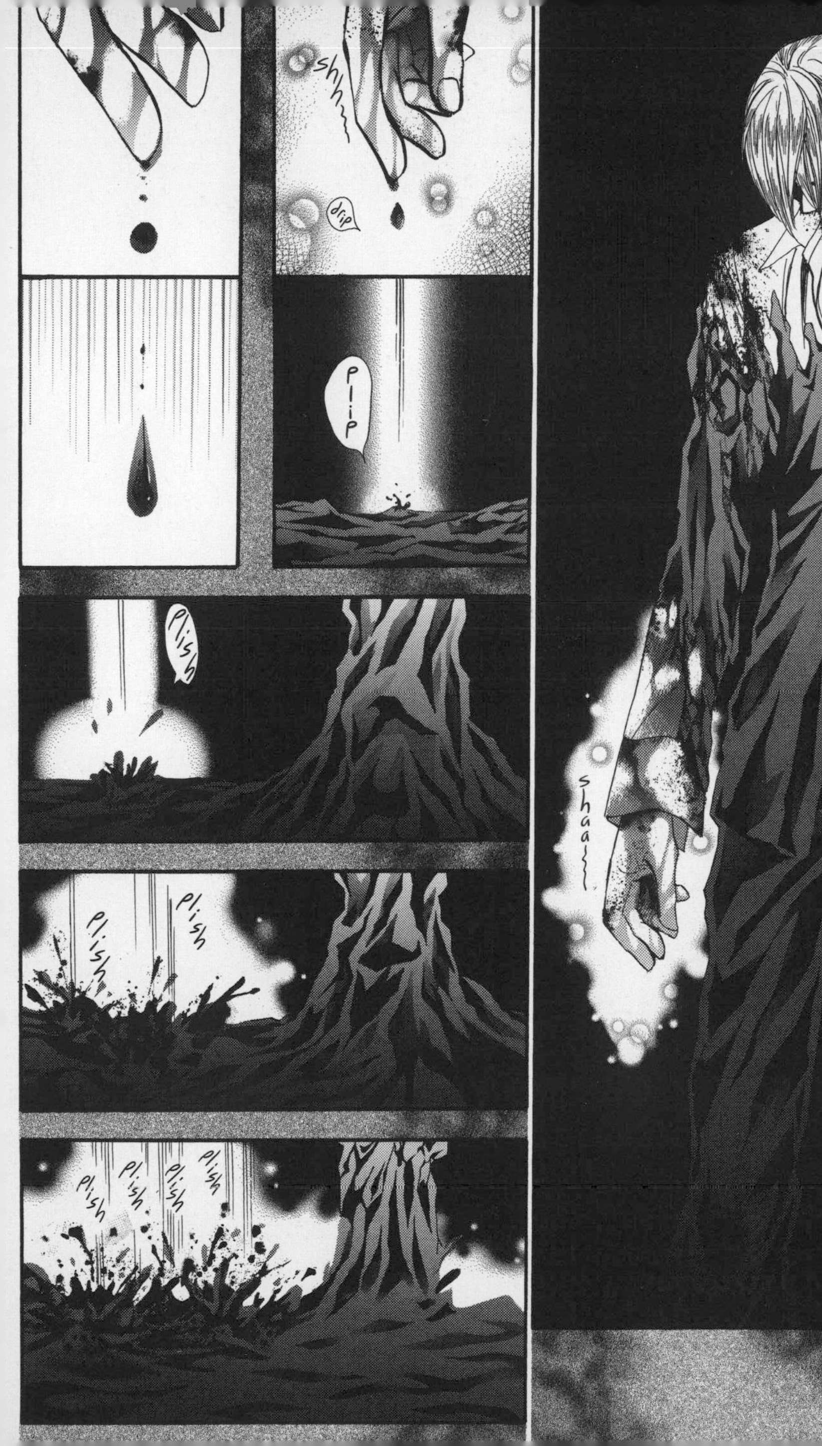
shhh
drip
plip
plish
plish
plish
plish
plish
plish
plish
shaa

sploosh
sploosh
sploosh
sploosh
sploosh
sploosh
sploosh
sploosh

...
MR....
...TSU-
RUGA
?!

ARE YOU ALL RIGHT?!
mrmr
mrmr
mrmr
mrmr
...
mrmr
mrmr
mrmr
mrmr
MR....
...TSU-RUGA?
...

CAN YOU...
...HEAR...
...ME?

mrmr
mrmr
mrmr
mrmr

MMM...

End of Act 166

Skip·Beat!
Act 167: Violence Mission, Phase 10

WILL I...
...BE CRUSHED TO PIECES AND DISAPPEAR?

I COULDN'T GO FORWARD ...
...OR RETREAT.
I WAS STUCK AND COULDN'T MOVE.
I...
...WAS PULLED OUT OF...
...THE DEPTHS OF THAT HORRIBLE DARKNESS...
MR....
...TSURUGA?

CAN YOU...
...HEAR...

...ME?

...BY
HER...
clasp

I...
...DIDN'T THINK...

...I'D BE TRAPPED AGAIN BY THE FEELINGS I HAD BACK THEN.
"WILL I...
...WITHER...
...AND DISAP-PEAR?"
THAT GIRL...
...WARDS OFF EVIL.
THE PRESIDENT...
...RESCUED ME...
...THEN...
WHEN YOU'RE STUCK AND CAN'T FREE YOURSELF ...
...SHE'S THE GOOD-LUCK CHARM WHO'LL TAKE YOU OUT OF THERE.

SHE'S ...
...THE STRONGEST GOOD-LUCK CHARM AVAILABLE TO YOU.
A "GOOD-LUCK CHARM"...
MAYBE...
...THIS IS WHY...
...THE PRESIDENT ASSIGNED HER TO ME.

HE...
...WASN'T WORRIED ABOUT ME EATING.
HE WAS WORRIED...
...THAT I'D BE TRAPPED BY KUON'S EMOTIONS AND FREEZE UP...
...
THAT'S VERY LIKELY.
YES.
I DON'T THINK HE FORESAW THE TROUBLE WITH THE CAR STUNT...
...BUT HE KNOWS THAT I'M...
...GOING TO HAVE TO FREE KUON, WHO I'VE KEPT LOCKED UP ALL THIS TIME.
HE WAS AFRAID I'D BE...
...DRAGGED DOWN BY KUON'S EMOTIONS WHILE PLAYING B.J. ...
...AND WOULDN'T BE ABLE TO RETURN...
...TO REN TSURUGA...

TSURUGA.
!
!
THANKS FOR WAITING.
YOU CAN GO HOME NOW.
UH ...
Electrocardiogram
I'M REALLY SORRY...
...FOR THIS DELAY IN THE SHOOTING ...
Heh
SHEESH, DON'T APOLO-GIZE TO ME SO MANY TIMES.
I'M JUST RELIEVED YOU WEREN'T HURT.
I mean it.
I WAS SCARED YOU MIGHT'VE HIT YOUR HEAD HARD.
I'm Glad there was nothing wrong.
Authorized Personnel Only
I'M SORRY.
AT THE TIME, I COULDN'T TELL THAT I WASN'T SEEING OR HEARING ANYTHING.
THAT'S HOW BIG THE SHOCK WAS.
Like the doctor said.
SOMETHING LIKE THAT RARELY HAPPENS UNDER NORMAL CIRCUM-STANCES.

I'M SURE YOU'VE NEVER DRIVEN LIKE THAT BEFORE.
...
DON'T WORRY ABOUT THE SCENE.
WE'LL SHOOT IT AGAIN ONCE WE CLEAR PERMISSION TO USE THAT STREET AGAIN.
...
UH.
THAT'S WHAT I **WISH** I COULD TELL YOU.

I...
...AGREE WITH THE DIRECTOR.
YOU HAVE TO START SHOOTING SOON AS CAIN HEEL...
...MAYBE BEFORE THE FINAL EPISODE OF DARK MOON WRAPS UP.
WE CAN'T AFFORD TO HAVE ANYTHING HAPPEN...
...SO YOU SHOULD AVOID ANY RISKS.
AREN'T YOU...

...THINKING THAT TOO?
...
YOU USUALLY SPEAK YOUR MIND ABOUT YOUR WORK...
...BUT YOU DIDN'T THIS TIME.
AND...
...DIRECTOR OGATA PROPOSED USING A STUNTMAN, WHICH GOES AGAINST YOUR PRINCIPLES.
PLEASE LET ME...
...THINK ABOUT IT TONIGHT...
...

HE COMPLIMENTED MY STUNT DRIVING.
EVEN I'M SCARED OF DOING IT AGAIN-
YEAH, IF YOU WANT TO PUT IT THAT WAY.
Though I don't accept that excuse, cuz I know something like that doesn't scare you at all.
SO.
NO MATTER THE REASON, YOU SHOULDN'T DO IT IF YOU'VE GOT DOUBTS...
...CUZ...
...MISTAKES DO HAPPEN...

...IF YOU'RE NOT MENTALLY PREPARED.
UH...
WHAT DID HE MEAN BY "EXPERT" ?
IT DOESN'T MATTER HOW MUCH OF AN "EXPERT" YOU ARE...
CHAK
HE COMPARED ME TO THE EXPERTS.
WHAT SORT OF DRIVING SKILLS DOES MR. YASHIRO THINK I HAVE?
"CUZ MIS-TAKES DO HAP-PEN."
I'M...

...NOT SCARED OF STUNT DRIVING.
WHAT I'M SCARED OF...
fwip
...IS...
...KUON'S DARKNESS THAT COULD SURFACE AT ANY TIME.
AND I DON'T KNOW WHAT WILL CAUSE IT TO HAPPEN...
fwump
tmp
I'VE LIVED...
...FOR YEARS AS REN TSURUGA...
...AND...
WHEN I RETURN TO REN TSURUGA...
...I SWITCH MODES...
...HAVE NEVER BEEN TAKEN OVER BY KUON'S EMOTIONS.
IS IT BECAUSE...
...I HAD TO WAKE UP KUON'S DARKNESS TO PLAY CAIN HEEL...
...EVEN BEFORE I GOT THE ROLE OF B.J.?

...AND PUT A LID ON KUON.
BUT THAT LID...
... SLIPPED DUE TO THE SHOCK.
I...
...CAN'T SEAL IT UP LIKE BEFORE...
...AND...
shfff
...I CAN'T CONTROL KUON WHEN HE WAKES UP ON HIS OWN.
...
THE NEXT TIME SOMETHING HAPPENS...
...WILL I BE AWARE OF IT?
WILL I BE ABLE TO CONTROL IT...
...BEFORE I GO BERSERK?
I'M...
...NOT SURE...

THE DARKNESS IN ME...
...IS FREE FROM ITS PRISON...
I'VE THOUGHT ABOUT THIS BEFORE...
Oh? It was...
Ping
A villainous
Underground broker
AH...
YES... IT WAS AFTER I TALKED WITH THE PRESIDENT...
...ABOUT WHETHER OR NOT I'D KEEP MS. MOGAMI... SETSU AS MY GOOD-LUCK CHARM...
...AND GUSHES OUT ON ITS OWN...
HMM?
WHEN SHE'S WITH ME...
...I NEARLY FORGET...
...WHAT I...
...MUST REMEMBER IN ORDER TO LIVE...

...BOTH OF THEM...
SQUEEZE
...ARE IMPORTANT...
TO ME...
HOWEVER...

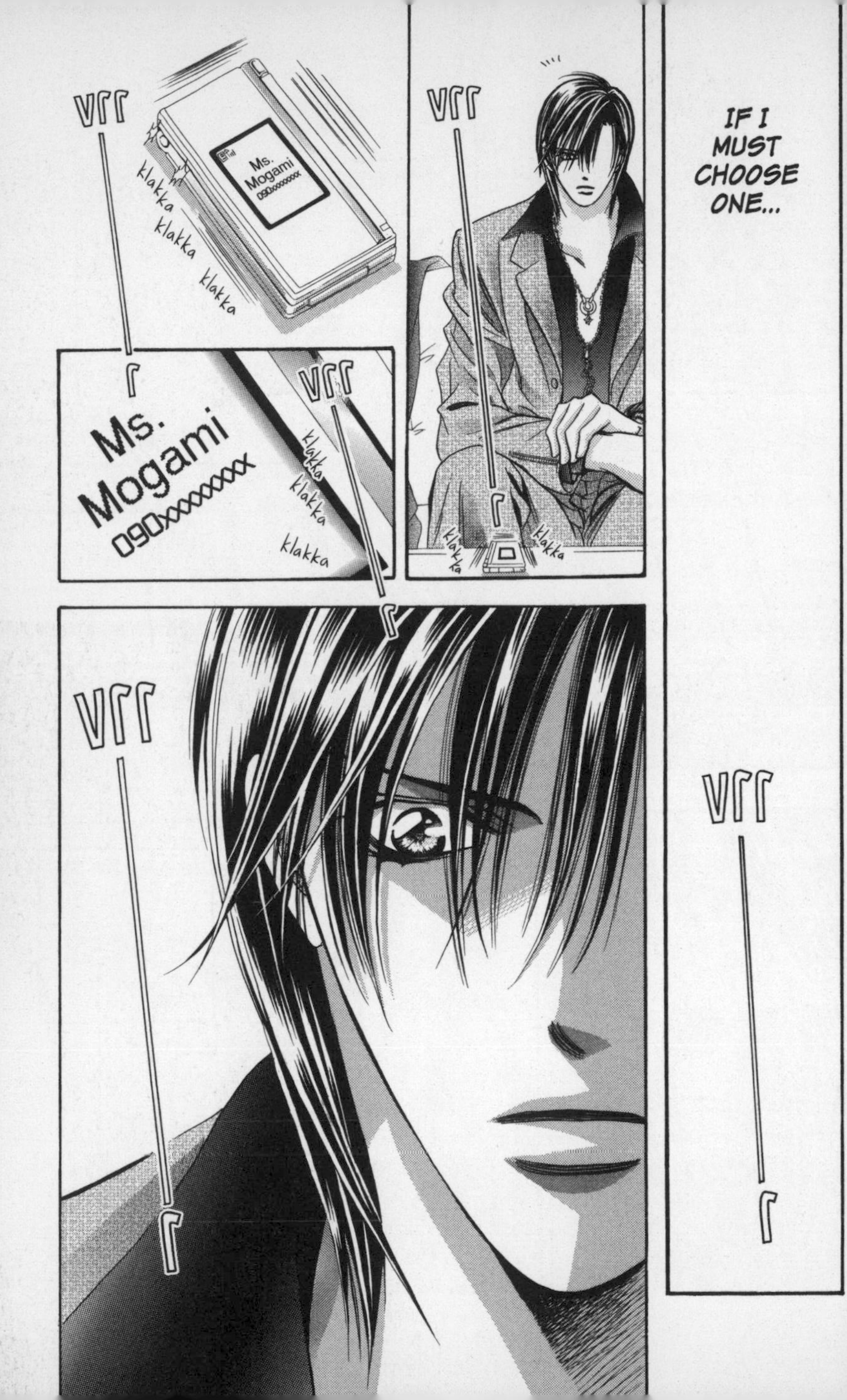
IF I MUST CHOOSE ONE...
Vrr
r
Vrr
r
klakka
klakka
klakka
Vrr
r
Ms. Mogami
090xxxxxxxx
klakka
klakka
klakka
Vrr
r
Ms. Mogami
090xxxxxxxx
klakka
klakka
klakka
Vrr
r

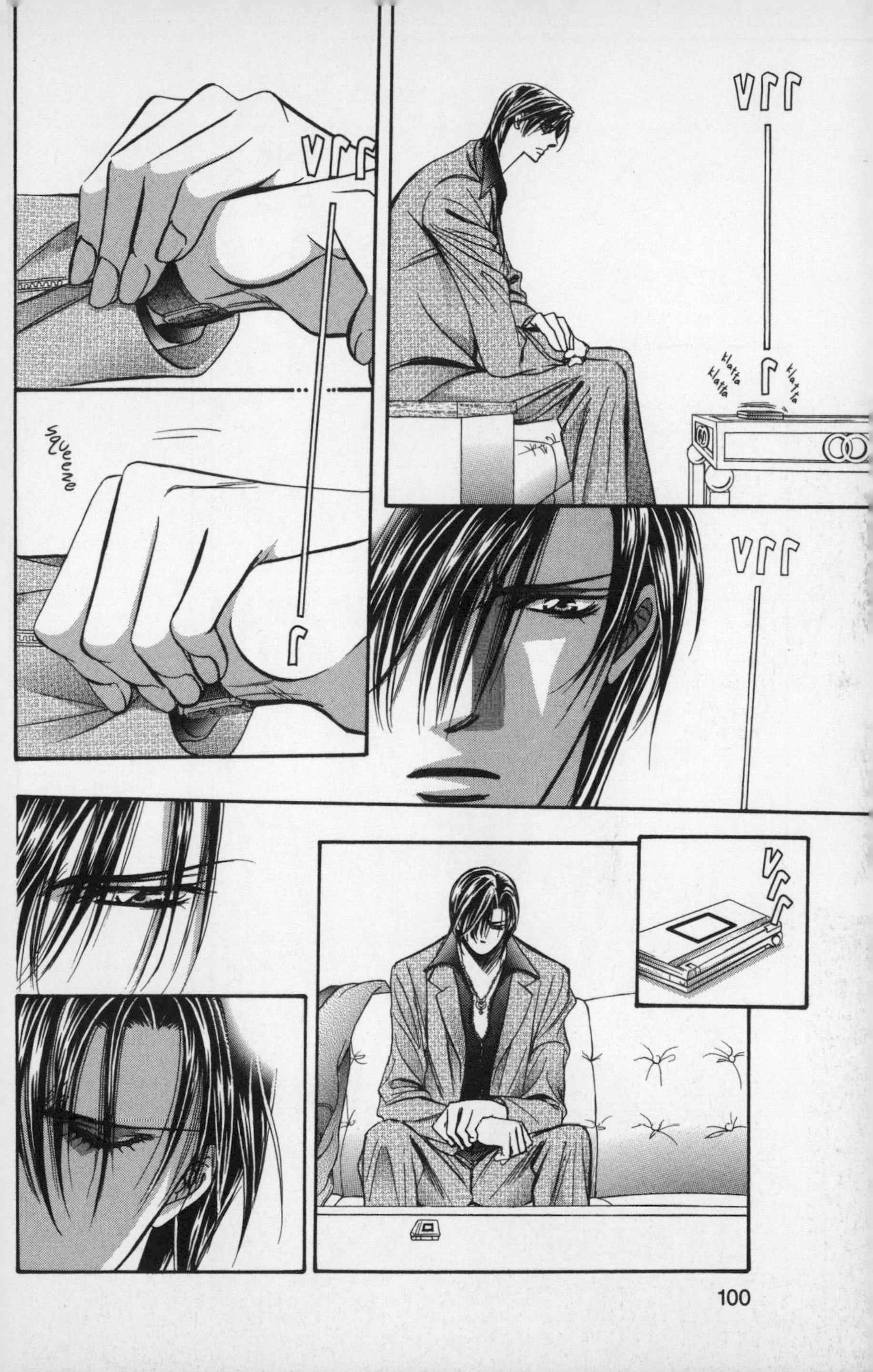
Vrrr
klatta
klatta
klatta
Vrrr
squeeze
Vrrr
Vrr

IS THAT...
...WHAT THE JAPANESE CALL "MORAL OBLIGATION"?
...SYMPATHY?
OR IS IT...

NO...
THAT'S NOT IT.
SORRY—
DON'T APOLO-GIZE.
THAT'S...
...NOT IT...
nuh uh
YOU KNOW...
...THAT I...
...HATE PEOPLE WHO DON'T LIVE THEIR LIVES FOR THEMSELVES.
YOU ONLY GET SO MUCH TIME ON EARTH.
IF YOU'VE GOT THE TIME TO STAND AROUND AND MOPE, GET OUT AND DO SOMETHING.
IF YOU FEEL GUILTY ABOUT ME...

...STAND UP...
...KUON.

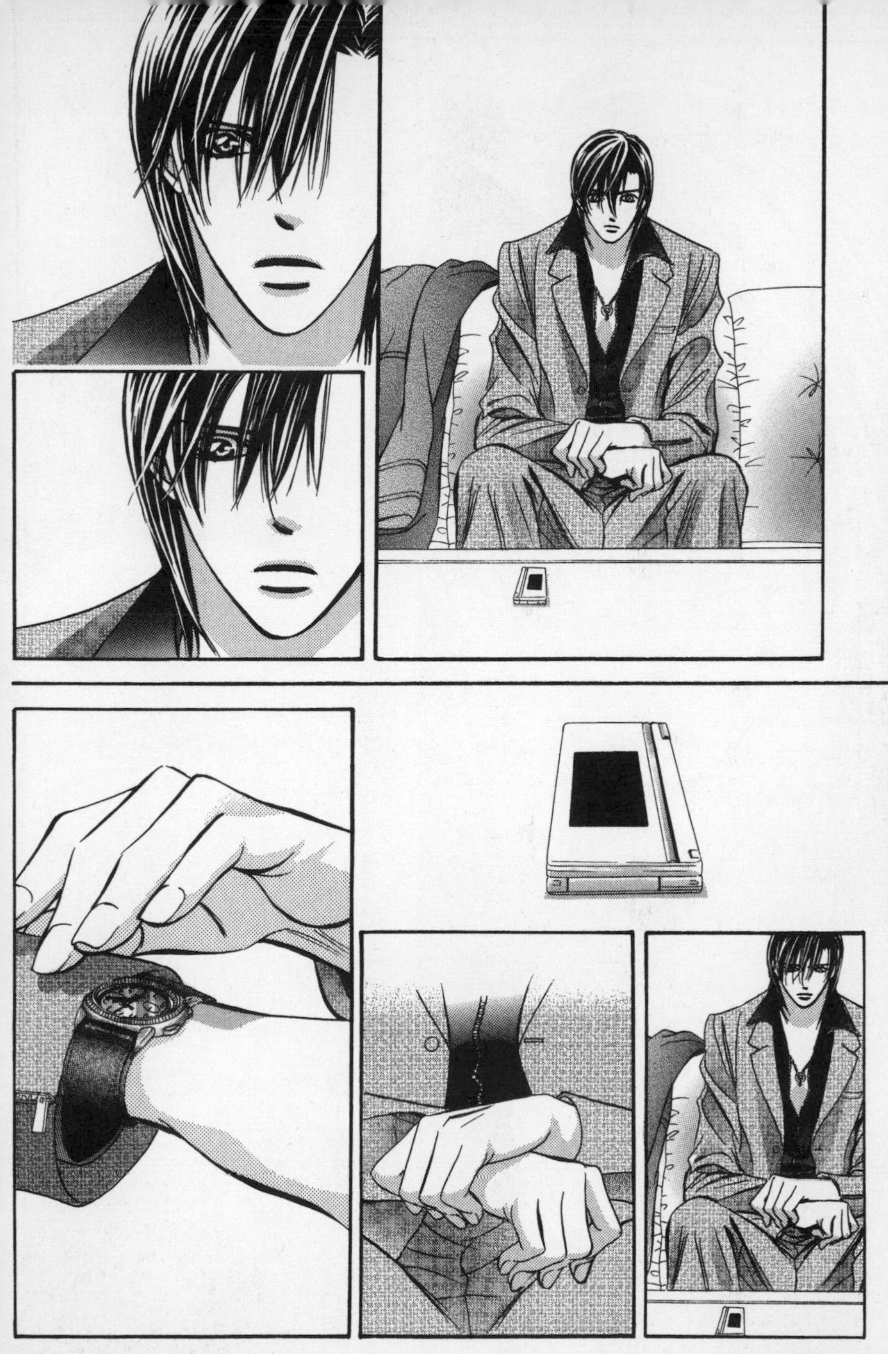

clak
HMM...
UH...
Hmm
NO NO...
clak
I WON'T.
HE DIDN'T ANSWER...
...SO MAYBE HE'S ALREADY ASLEEP.
From sedatives or something.
I SHOULDN'T WAKE HIM UP...
Oh!
...
chak
M-MAYBE...

...HE'S BEEN HOSPITALIZED BECAUSE HE SUDDENLY GOT WORSE?!
HIS ANSWERING SERVICE WAS OFF...
...Oh!...
BUT ...
It'd be on if he was in the hospital ...
Oh!
M-MAYBE ...
HE COLLAPSED SOMEWHERE ALONE?!
A lonely Mr. Tsuruga
The last scene
M...
MR. YASHIRO!
Yes!
MR. YASHIRO MUST'VE ACCOMPANIED HIM TO THE HOSPITAL!
FWIK
WHAT ON EARTH HAS HAPPENED TO MR. TSURUAGA, MR. YASHIRO?!
Give me the Mr. Tsuruga news! The Mr. Tsuruga news fla sh!
Yikes!
!

Wah!
Wah!
Incoming Call
Calling
Mr. Tsuruga

End of Act 167

Skip·Beat!
Act 168: Violence Mission, Phase 10.5

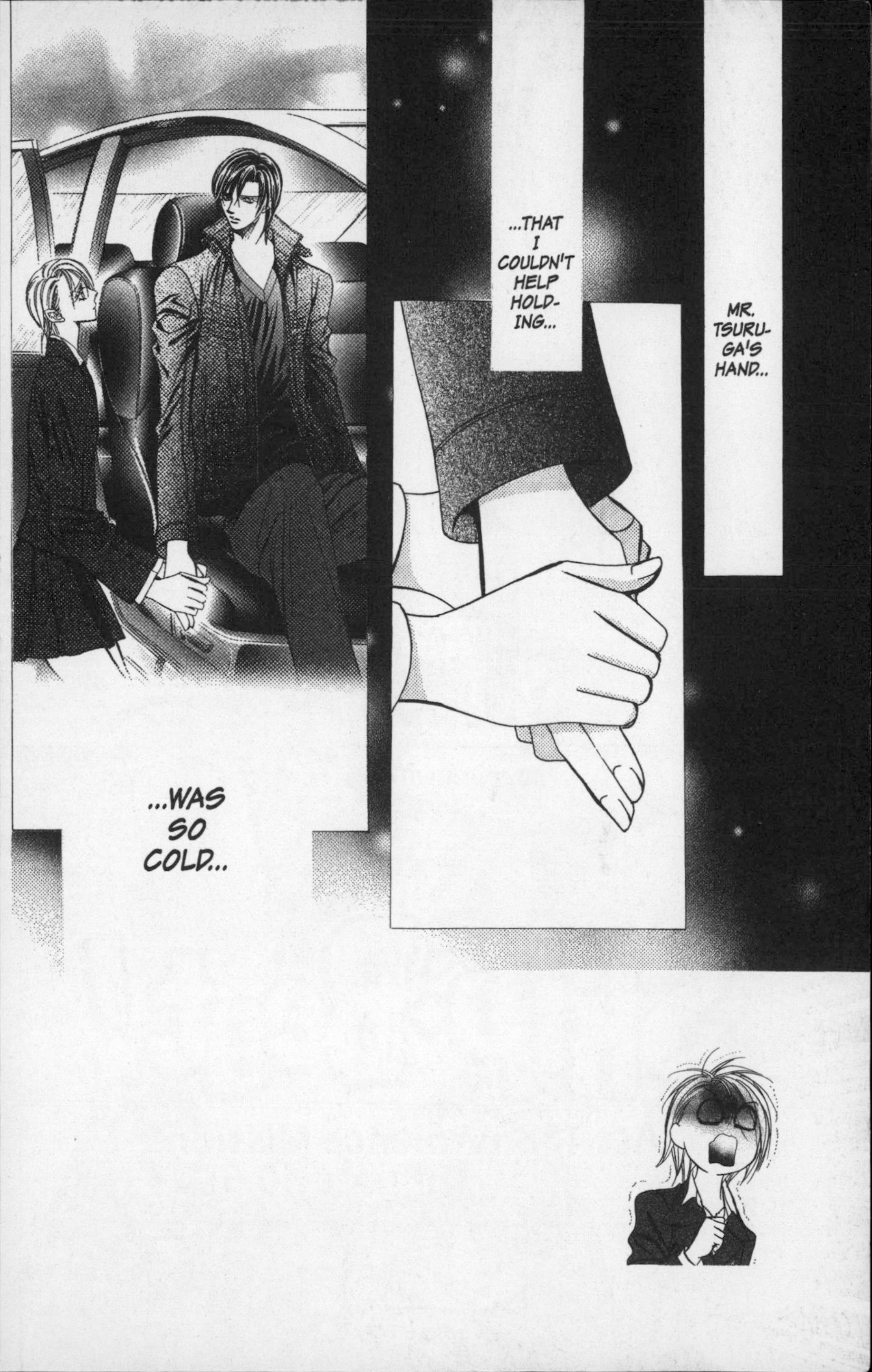
MR. TSURUGA'S HAND...
...THAT I COULDN'T HELP HOLDING...
...WAS SO COLD...

WHY...
...AM I DOING THIS?
Shopping with Mr. Tsuruga
in a high-end supermarket
THESE ITEMS, EVEN THE CHEAP ONES, COST TWICE AS MUCH AS IN A REGULAR SUPER-MARKET...
thr thump thr thump
nervous
fidget
HMM.
FROZEN
I'M NOT COMFORTABLE AT ALL... I WON'T LOOK AT ANYTHING...
I CAN'T TELL WHICH CHICKEN IS BETTER.

NOOOO!
HE'S ACTING LIKE A STEREO-TYPICAL RICH DUDE!
WELL, THE EXPENSIVE ONE MUST BE BETTER.
Can't go wrong with that.
I'LL TAKE THE HIGH-GRADE ONE.
toss
M...
Mr. Tsuruga...
E-E-E-Excuse me for butting in...
If you ignore the brand and simply look at the quality, the cheaper one is fresher and is a better deal!
HUH?
EVEN IF IT'S CHEAPER?
Uh-huh!
Yes!
HOW CAN YOU TELL?
IT'S FIRMER, YOUNGER, SHINIER AND THE COLOR IS BETTER!
JUST LIKE HUMANS, THE YOUNGER THE CHICKEN IS, THE MORE PLUMP AND SHINY IT IS!
If the skin's still on, the goose bumps look great!
They both...
HMM...
...look the same to me...
Well... All right.
I'LL TAKE THIS ONE THEN.
THE FRESHER THE BETTER.
I can't taste the difference anyway.
La la la
UH...TO A COMMONER LIKE ME, BOTH OF THEM ARE OUT OF REACH...
The cheaper one is expensive enough already.

rustle
Thank you.
tmp
tmp
tmp
tmp

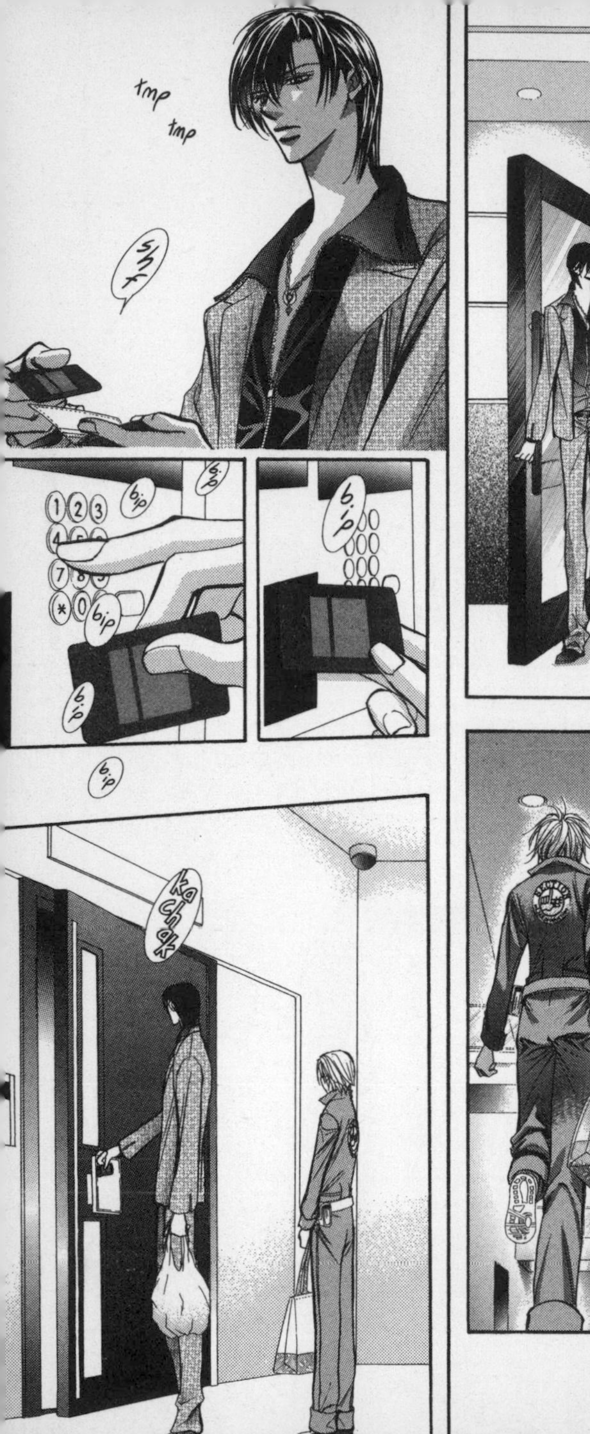
tmp
tmp
shf
bip
bip
bip
bip
bip
kachak

PLEASE, COME IN.
※ Mr. Tsuruga's apartment building and the expensive super-market are connected through the basement.
THANK YOU...
...
WHY
...
...AM I DOING THIS?
It's 11 PM.
IT'S ALL BECAUSE
...
...OF WHAT HAPPENED A LITTLE WHILE AGO.

Vrr
Incoming Call
Calling
Mr. Tsuruga
Mr. Tsuruga
Click
HELLO.
IT'S MOGAMI.
Ah.

Sorry.
I...
...couldn't answer the phone when you called me earlier.
OH.
IT'S ALL RIGHT.
PLEASE DON'T WORRY ABOUT IT.
U...
UM...
ARE YOU... STILL...
...AT THE HOSPITAL?
No.
I'm fine. I'm home.
I had a checkup and they found nothing wrong with me.
REALLY?
I'M SO GLAD...
Sorry for making you worry...
NO...
I'M...
You...

...warmed my cold body. I don't know how to thank you for it...

Don't say "body"!

I only warmed your HAND!

WHY DOES HE HAVE TO REFER TO IT IN SUCH A LECHEROUS WAY?!

WHY DO YOU NEED TO PUT THINGS THAT WAY WHEN I ONLY WARMED YOUR HAND!

YOU COULD'VE SIMPLY SAID "THANK YOU"!

Ah, you're right.

Yes yes.

Sorry sorry.

Thank you.

Heh

.....

I... I...

You don't need to thank me so formally...

I ONLY DID IT CUZ YOUR HAND WAS SO COLD...

SO I THOUGHT YOU MUST BE COLD...
Yes...
I was...
...very cold...
...
Ms. Mogami.
YES?
I've... got a favor to ask you...
WHAT IS IT?
Um.
Well.
It's some-thing very simple.
I...

...sud-denly feel like eating Oahu omelet rice.
That's it.
HUH?
Oahu?
I really searched for it...
I LOOKED IT UP...
SNAP
...UNTIL MR. TSURUGA CAME TO PICK ME UP.

THE OMELET RICE OF OAHU!
I've never eaten or seen one. I never knew such a thing existed.
THE IMAGE I FINALLY FOUND IS OF OMELET RICE THAT A JAPANESE RESTAURANT IN OAHU SERVES.
click click click
BUT I COULDN'T FIND THE RECIPE, EVEN THOUGH I SEARCHED ALL OVER FOR IT!
WHAT SORT OF DISH IS OAHU OMELET RICE?
IS IT DIFFERENT FROM JAPANESE OMELET RICE? IS IT TROPICAL?
Like with fruit sauce on it?
BUT MR. TSURUGA BOUGHT STUFF FOR MAKING ORDINARY CHICKEN OMELET RICE...
Can't be...
Oh? But he bought frozen shrimp too... oh?!
SORRY TO KEEP YOU WAITING, MS. MOGAMI.
jump
!
clack
LET'S BEGIN.
...
Y...
Uh...
YEEEEES.

WHAM
roll roll
in pieces

Mr. Tsuruga, the chef
HUUUUUH?!
WHAM WHAM
WHAM WHAM
in pieces
A...
SECTION
in L.M.E production
ARE YOU GONNA MAKE IT?!
And I was wondering why you suddenly served me coffee!
M...
SHUPP
H-HE'S WILD!
...
WHAT IS IT?
RIP RIP
toss
toss
M-M-M-Mr. Tsu-ruga...
Um... um...
AAAH!!
panic
panic
jitter
jitter
HMM?
RRIP
Chicken
U...
Um...

...What...
...should I do?
HMM?
AH.
HE SAID HE WANTED "TO EAT" IT, SO I ASSUMED I'D BE COOKING...
I'LL NEED YOUR HELP A LITTLE LATER.
toss
Frozen shrimp & chicken & vegetables
& rice
shup
HUH?!
A-ALL THAT AT ONCE?!
KYAAAAAAAH!
YELLOW SAND! I CAN'T SEE THE FOOD BECAUSE OF THE YELLOW SAND, MR. TSURUGA!
shiver
SO SIT TIGHT AND WAIT A BIT.
Salt and pepper
shk shk shk
shoom shoom
AH, I PUT TOO MUCH SEASONING IN. I'LL JUST ADD MORE RICE.
H-HOW DYNAM-IC!
WHAM WHAM
How many people is he cooking for?!
shup shup
shk shk
I'LL ADD MORE EGGS TO BALANCE OUT THE RICE.
IT'S TOO MUCH! JUST TOO MUCH! YOU'RE GONNA FOLD ALL THAT UP?!
WHAM WHAM
The eggs are almost scrambled!

GOOD.
BAM
IT'S DONE.
You can see the plate here and there.
Ah.
IT'S A WHOLE LOT BETTER THAN THE LAST TIME I MADE IT.
I CAN COOK A LOT BETTER THE SECOND TIME AROUND.
dazed
...
He cooked by brute force...
Eggs: Not quite folded. More like they were pressed together.
Tah dah!
Takamaru
DELICIOUS!
Organic ketchup
HERE.
NOW ...
...I'LL NEED YOUR HELP.
Y...

Takamaru
DELICIOUS!
Organic
ketchup
Ketchup on omelet rice...
YES?
...means...
SQUEEEEE...
...ZE
I'M DONE...
GOOD.
PERFECT.
Mr. Tsuruga's Request
"My lucky number, eight."
THE "8" LOOKS BEAUTIFUL.
And huge.
NOW.

LET'S DEFEAT IT!
tmp
Let's go to the living room, cuz it's more comfortable there.
...
MR. TSURUGA ...
Excuse me...
UM... WAS I...
BUT THIS IS ALL I'VE DONE TONIGHT!
...SUMMONED JUST FOR THIS?
NO WAY.
NO HUMAN BEING WOULD SUMMON SOMEONE LATE AT NIGHT JUST FOR THIS.
NOW HURRY.
LET US CONQUER THIS MONSTER WHILE IT'S HOT.
Monster?
YOU MADE IT...
Well I won't refute you, but...
...

MR. TSURUGA ...
THERE'S DEFINITELY ...
...SOMETHING WRONG WITH HIM...
I WAS ...
...FLABBER-GASTED THAT HE COOKED FOR HIMSELF...
...BUT HAVING HIM WANT TO EAT SOMETHING AT ALL IS ABNORMAL ...

"ABNORMAL"...
MAY-BE...
...WHAT-EVER AFFECTED HIM AFTER THAT STUNT...
...IS...
...STILL AFFECTING HIM...
I CAN'T DENY IT...
CUZ...
...HE...
...MUST'VE BEEN...
ALL...
...HIS SENSES...
...FROZE UP...
...TER-RIFIED.
...AND HE LOOKED SO PALE...
I'D BE...
...FRIGHT-ENED...
FRIGHT-ENED...
...AND...
Peek

JOLT
STARE
!
?!
Yes?!
YOU'RE NOT EATING?
Uh
MAYBE YOU DON'T LIKE OMELET RICE?
Wha ?!
No! No!
I Love omelet rice!
It's an executive of Mogami Favorite Foods Ltd.!!
The president is a hamburger steak with a fried egg on it.
I was...
...just thinking about something else.
I'm sorry.
I'll eat it now!
shak
CRUNCH
Egg layer
An unbelievable sound
I'LL ...
...EAT IT!

chomp
chew
blanch
IT...
HOW IS IT?
JOLT
!
GYAAOOO
IT'S A MONSTER!
TEXTURE
OO
TASTE
SECTION
LME production

...
GULP
...
I...
I LIKE IT...
WHAT ?
I...
I LIKE-
WHAT?

It's ...
The wand of misfortune
...full of originality and very... fantastic!
shiver
SOB
shake shake
bfft
?!
Heh heh heh heh
...DON'T NEED TO FORCE YOURSELF TO PRAISE IT...
YOU CAN BE HONEST AND SAY, "THIS TASTES AWFUL."
HOW CAN I?!
When Mr. Tsuruga cooked it himself!
...
YOU ...
Heh heh
THERE'S NO WAY YOU CAN HONESTLY SAY THIS TASTES GOOD.

I COOKED IT, SO IT TASTES WICKEDLY AWFUL.
?!
...
Y-YOU MEAN...
Um...
YOU COOKED IT SO IT TASTES AW—
...NOT GOOD...
UH.
Well.
THIS IS MY LEVEL OF KITCHEN EXPERTISE.
dig
dig
BUT EVEN THOUGH I HARDLY EVER COOK...
...WHEN I DO, I DO RESEARCH AND TRY MY BEST TO MAKE SOMETHING EDIBLE.
I WOULDN'T COOK SOMETHING THIS DESTRUCTIVE.
This is how it came out the first time, when I had no idea how to make it.
lumpy
AH.
CHOMP
YOU TOOK SUCH A BIG BITE...

CRUMPLE...
THIS IS AWFUL ...

HUH?
Aw...?
THE OAHU OMELET RICE...

...WAS ACTUALLY AN "AWFUL OMELET RICE."
Apparently.
WHEN YOU EAT IT, YOU CAN'T SWALLOW IT RIGHT AWAY...
...SO THE "AWFUL" SOUNDS LIKE "OAHU", HENCE THE NAME...
OMELET RICE WAS CREATED IN JAPAN...
...SO OAHU WOULD ONLY HAVE JAPANESE-STYLE OMELET RICE.
Well, they could've come up with some sort of original omelet rice.
I THOUGHT IT WAS SOMETHING LIKE LOCO MOCO...
SO.
WE TALKED ABOUT OMELET RICE...
...WHILE CONTINUING TO SHOVE DOWN MR. TSURUGA'S "OAHU" OMELET RICE.
EXHAUSTED
AWFUL ...
MS. MO-GAMI ...
YOU DON'T NEED TO FINISH YOURS.
THAT'S...

...WHAT MR. TSURUGA TOLD ME.
Mountain of Death
I'M ON THE DESCENT NOW!
Half left
WHAT'RE YOU SAYING?
SECTION LME inLMEproduction
LET'S DO OUR BEST!
WHEN YOU'RE ABOUT TO GIVE IN DURING AN EMERGENCY, YOU CAN'T SURVIVE UNLESS YOU CHEER ON THE PERSON NEXT TO YOU!

I COULDN'T JUST...
...SIT BACK AND WATCH HIM...
...CUZ...
...MR. TSURUGA...
...WAS EATING...
...LIKE HE WAS FIGHTING SOME-THING...

End of Act 168

Skip·Beat!
Act 169: Violence Mission, Phase 11

THIS...
...IS YOU...
FWAP FWAP
FWAP FWAP

FWAP
FWAP
...KUON.
IT'S A CHICKEN.
I'M TELLING YOU, THAT CHICKEN HEART OF YOURS IS YOUR WEAKNESS.
GROW BIG, BRIAN.
DON'T TAKE CARE OF IT!
And don't name it!
WHAT'RE YOU GONNA DO IF IT GETS BIGGER?!
It's already full-grown!
peck peck

DUDE, TAKE THAT CHICKEN...
...THROTTLE IT, POUND IT, CRUSH IT WITH YOUR OWN HANDS...
...SHOVE IT DOWN YOUR THROAT WITH YOUR CHICKEN HEART AND SHIT IT ALL OUT!
...
cluck
DON'T YOU DARE CRY!
Are you already attached to it?!
THEY TAKE ADVANTAGE OF YOU BECAUSE YOU'RE SO NICE... SO PITIFUL.
IF YOU FIGHT BACK, YOU CAN BEAT THEM UP NO PROBLEM.
MY DAD AND SENSEI SAY MARTIAL ARTS SHOULDN'T BE USED TO HURT PEOPLE...
I KNOW THAT!

IF YOU GET IN TROUBLE, YOU'RE GONNA MAKE THINGS HARD ON YOUR MOM AND DAD...
...SO YOU KEEP YOUR MOUTH SHUT AND PUT UP WITH ALL THAT CRAP.
BUT...
...YOU'RE GOING TO END UP DESTROY-ING YOURSELF.
YOU DON'T MIND...
...WHEN THEY STEAL ALL THE PLACES WHERE YOU CAN BREATHE?
THAT WHAT YOU WANT?
YOU WON'T MIND NOT BEING ABLE TO ACT ANYMORE?
peck
peck

peck peck
clench
I'LL EAT IT...

CHICKEN
NUGGET
UH.
WHO TOLD YOU TO GET THIS?!
IT'S OKAY. IT'S CHICKEN.
IT'S NOT OKAY!
Brian's still alive
peck peck

I told you.

YOU NEED TO CONQUER IT BY CRUSHING IT WITH YOUR OWN HANDS AND FLAMING IT YOURSELF!

IT'S NO GOOD IF YOU EAT SOMETHING THAT'S BEEN COOKED FOR YOU!

ALL RIGHT...

...

I'LL BUY SOME CHICKEN AND "CONQUER" IT MY OWN WAY...

"Conquered"

steam

steam

steam

WHAT IS THAT?
COAL?
IT'S A DELICIOUS DISH CALLED OMELET RICE. YOU STIR-FRY RICE, VEGGIES, SHRIMP, AND CHICKEN, AND FOLD THEM UP IN AN OMELET.
Dad made it a couple times for me.
HMM...
Doesn't look "delicious" at all...
I MADE IT JUST LIKE DAD DOES.
IT DOESN'T LOOK GOOD, BUT SHOULD TASTE GOOD.
CRUNCH
An unbelievable sound
chomp
VILE, DREADFUL, FOUL... JUST LIKE A MONSTER.
THAT'S GOOD.
LUNGE
Uh
HEY!
Wait!
DON'T THROW IT AWAY!
IT'S AW-FUL...
AWFUL, HUH?
Why? I made it just like Dad did...
AN "AWFUL" ENEMY IS ONE WORTH CONQUERING.

DON'T LOSE TO IT. EAT IT ALL.
But scrape off the carcinogenic shell first.
...
I'VE BEEN THINKING.
IF I EAT THIS, IT'LL GET ABSORBED INTO MY FLESH AND BLOOD...
...SO THE CHICKEN WILL STILL BE PART OF ME.
AH.
THEN YOU NEED TO TRANSFORM THIS "EVIL CHICKEN" INTO "POWERFUL CHICKEN" SO WHEN IT BECOMES YOUR FLESH AND BLOOD, IT GIVES YOU STRENGTH.
IT'S EASY.
RICK...
HAVE THE WOMAN YOU LOVE PUT A SPELL ON IT.
LIKE, "YOU CAN DO IT." "YOU CAN WIN FOR SURE."
GOT IT?
.....
WHAT'S WITH YOU?
WHY SO GLUM?

...

MIRANDA DUMPED ME...

I DON'T HAVE ANYONE TO PUT A SPELL ON IT FOR ME...

HUH? YOU GOT DUMPED AGAIN?

MIRANDA DROPPED YOU FASTER THAN LORRAINE DID.

I HOPE YOU'RE TREATING THEM RIGHT, IF YOU KNOW WHAT I MEAN.

Are you a chicken there, too?

...

WELL...

NO COMPLAINTS ABOUT **THAT**, BUT FOR SOME REASON...

...THEY STILL LEAVE ME...

GLOOM

...

SHEESH...

FINE... THIS TIME I'LL DO IT.

I'LL USE A SECRET SPELL THAT'S BEEN HANDED DOWN IN MY FAMILY.

YOU BETTER BE GRATEFUL FOR THIS.

TINA'S THE ONLY ONE I'VE EVER DONE THIS FOR.

kachak

HEY, WHAT CAN I WRITE ON THAT WITH?

KETCHUP.

COOL.

POP

SHAA
...SO HE CAN BE...
...HAPPY FOR ALL TIME...
HAPPINESS, COME AGAIN.
BRING GOOD LUCK WITH YOU...
...AND STAY BY KUON'S SIDE...
SHPLORT

clench
SECTION

COLLAPSE...
ABOUT TO DIE
Oh!
The Grim Reaper
225
224
mumble mumble
Count-down to his death
M-MR. TSU-RUGA...
GET AHOLD OF YOUR-SELF.
Um...
I BROUGHT SOME ANTACIDS FOR YOU.
210

PLEASE TAKE THEM...
WHY NOT?
...
YOU ...
... DON'T WANT THEM?
YOU MUST BE SUFFERING...
...
I'LL...
...DI-GEST IT...
...MY-SELF ...
OR...
...I'LL LOSE.

THAT'S HOW I FEEL...
...
ALL RIGHT.
BUT...
...LET ME KNOW IF IT GETS REALLY BAD.
I'LL HAVE THE ANTACID RIGHT HERE, JUST IN CASE.
clink
UH...
clink
clank

IT'S ALL RIGHT...
...MS. MOGA-MI.
JUST LEAVE IT...
LET ME AT LEAST CLEAN UP.
YOU'VE ALREADY COOKED. IF YOU'RE GONNA DO THE DISHES AS WELL...
...I DON'T UNDERSTAND WHY I CAME OVER.
GIVE ME...
...AN EXCUSE AT LEAST.
...
THANKS...

THEN... PLEASE...
Hey hey hey~~, you the Grim Reaper?!
You should be prepared to die when you fight us~~!
ANGER
ANGER
ANGER
Thrashing the Grim Reaper
MR. TSURUGA...
...DID THIS...
ksss—h
clink
clink
clank
clank
...FOR GOOD LUCK?
I'VE HEARD THAT ATHLETES DO THAT SORT OF THING...
LIKE EATING STEAK AND PORK CUTLET TO WIN AGAINST THE ENEMY...
splish
splish
clink
clink
SO...
...

THE "CHICKEN OMELET RICE" THAT MR. TSURUGA COOKED...
THERE WAS SHRIMP IN IT, BUT...
Well...
"CHICKEN" ...
..."WIMP"...
...CAN MEAN...
SKWIK
SKWIK
...OR "COWARD."
I...
...THOUGHT...
SKWIK
...MAYBE...
BUT...
MR. TSURUGA IS DIFFERENT FROM ME...
...SO THAT CAN'T BE WHAT HE'S DOING.
BUT...

HE FROZE ...
...LIKE THAT.
MAYBE...
clink
...HE'S SCARED.
EVEN IF HE IS MR. TSURUGA...
SO SCARED ...
...I'D HESITATE...
I'D...
...BE SCARED ...
...THE CAR CHASE AGAIN...
...TO DO...

IT'S EASY.
HAVE THE WOMAN YOU LOVE PUT A SPELL ON IT.
Heh
I...
...DON'T BELIEVE IN MAGIC...
I REALLY DON'T.
BUT I NEEDED SOME MOMENTUM.
WHEN SHE'S WITH ME...

...I'M TER-RIFIED ...
...I'M ABOUT TO FORGET ABOUT RICK.
BUT...
...I NEED HER...
...SO THAT MY DARK-NESS DOESN'T TAKE OVER.
I RUN AWAY...
...BECAUSE I CAN'T CHOOSE.
VRR
VRR
VRR
BUT...
...I NEED MOMENTUM...
...SO I DON'T HESITATE TO CHARGE DOWN THE PATH I'VE CHOSEN...
...AND I NEED THE WILL-POWER TO MAKE IT HAPPEN ...

...WANT TO DO MY WORK...

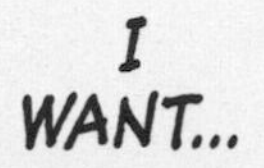

THAT'S...

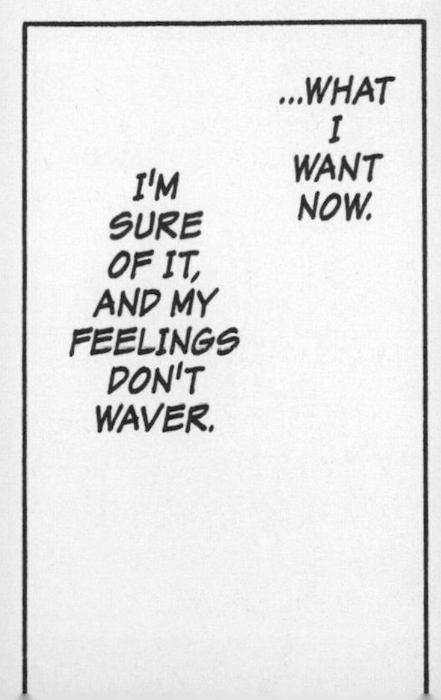

TO MAKE THAT HAPPEN...
...I...
...HAVE TO WIN AGAINST MYSELF.
YOU CAN DO IT.
YOU CAN WIN FOR SURE.
"I'LL BELIEVE...
...IN WHAT I CAN DO."

SO I'LL FIGHT ...
... WITH ALL I'VE GOT!
I'LL BELIEVE ...
...IN WHAT I CAN DO!
MY POSSI-BILITIES ...
...ARE...
...INFINITE.
I...
...DON'T THINK YOU SHOULD LIMIT YOUR-SELF...
...MR. TSU-RUGA.
Oh!

WHAT?
I THOUGHT MAYBE I SHOULDN'T WAKE YOU UP...
...BUT I DECIDED TO ANYWAY, BECAUSE I HAVE SOMETHING VERY IMPORTANT TO TELL YOU.
Sorry...
NO... IT'S OKAY...
I WASN'T ASLEEP...
What?
Oh.
REALLY?
Good.
SO, WHAT IS THIS VERY IMPORTANT THING?
UH...
TO BE HONEST, I'M NOT SURE ABOUT DOING THIS...
...TO YOU, WHO GAVE ME THIS...
...SOMETIMES YOU JUST CAN'T CHANGE THE WAY YOU FEEL ABOUT SOMETHING.
AND I'VE OFTEN HAD MAGICAL HELP AT TIMES LIKE THAT...
U...
WELL...
UM...
UH...
?
BUT...
Well...
YOU DENY THAT IT'S POSSIBLE...

...but I've had other people ...
...give me miraculous words like "mature" and "beautiful" when I become Natsu...
AH.
YOU MEAN THE PRIN-CESS ROSA?
THAT'S NOT MAGIC.
BLUNT
It's not magic at all.
SO BLUNT
...
YOU MUST EXPER-IENCE IT...
...IN ORDER TO BELIEVE IT.
jangle

I FEEL INVINCIBLE...
...WHEN PRINCESS ROSA IS WITH ME.
NO MATTER HOW WEAK I FEEL...
...EVEN IF THINGS SEEM INSURMOUNTABLE...
...SHE MAKES IT POSSIBLE.
HAVE THE WOMAN YOU LOVE...
...PUT A SPELL ON IT.
SO...
...YOU SHOULD BE ABLE TO DO IT TOO.
YOU CAN DO IT.

EVEN IF YOU ENCOUNTER TROUBLE AGAIN...
...YOU'LL BE ABLE TO WIN THIS TIME.
YOU CAN WIN FOR SURE.
PUT ASIDE YOUR DOUBTS...
... AND ...
...BE WITH HER...

SHE'S THE STRONG-EST...
...GOOD-LUCK CHARM AVAILABLE.

ALL RIGHT...
!
I'LL BE...
...WITH HER...
End of Act 169

It...

...was never meant to be opened.

Skip·Beat!
Act 170: Violence Mission, Phase 12

A journey to the gold desert and the pyramids!
Mys-teries!
A journey for two!
And you get to stay at a luxurious three-star hotel!
No.
stamp stamp
fwip
Why not?!

IF SHE GETS THAT PRIZE, AND IT'S MORE EXPENSIVE THAN MS. MOMOSE'S AND OTHER SENIOR ACTORS' PRIZES, WHAT'RE YOU GOING TO DO?
It's more expensive for sure.
WE ALREADY GOT A QSQ GAME CONSOLE FOR MS. MOGAMI.
So not to worry.
THEN HOW ABOUT REN?
Tch
Since you get to stay at a luxurious three-star hotel.
GNH ...
YOU DON'T NEED TO WORRY ABOUT HIM. HE'S NOT A TEENAGER EXPERIENCING THE "RAFFLE" AT THE AFTER-PARTY...
...FOR THE FIRST TIME LIKE MS. MOGAMI.
AH.
Yeah.
By the way...
MATSUSHIMA WAS BOASTING THAT REN TOLD HIM "I EXPLORED NEW TERRITORY IN DARK MOON...
"...SO CAN I CHOOSE THE PRIZE?"
A while back.
HE MENTIONED PICKING AN OVERSEAS TRAVEL PACKAGE.
HMM.
OH. I WAS THINKING ABOUT MAKING HIM CHANGE HIS PRIZE IF IT WAS A CHEAP ONE.
To the Egypt vacation.

WELL, ALL RIGHT.
fwip
I'LL DO SOMETHING ABOUT THIS MYSELF.
PRESI-DENT.
DO NOT CRASH THE PARTY.
FREEZE
HOW DARE YOU ...?!
I'D NEVER DO SOME-THING LIKE THAT.
KNOWING YOU, YOU'D TURN THE VENUE INTO A DESERT WITHOUT PERMIS-SION.
Complete with the pyramids, the sphinx, and camels.
HOW DARE YOU?
GOOD TO HEAR IT.
IF YOU ATTEND, THE TONE OF THE PARTY WILL MORPH...
...FROM "FAREWELL DARK MOON" TO "LORY TAKARADA PRESENTS A PARTY THAT COMPLETELY IGNORES COMMON SENSE!"
I'D NEVER DO SOMETHING OUT-RAGEOUS LIKE THAT.

I'LL BE MODEST, AND JUST TAKE A PEEK WITH CLEOPATRA※ AND TUTANKHAMEN※.
※ Cosplay by super-beautiful/handsome foreigners
SO YOU WERE PLANNING TO GO.
And you call that modest?
tmp
tmp
tmp
tmp
HMM?
OH.
THAT BACK, STANDING SO NEEDLESSLY STRAIGHT. IT'S...

HEY...
?

H...
...ey.
KYOKO.
WHAT—
WHY DO YOU LOOK SO DOWN?
I couldn't help asking, cuz you look so ridiculous.
JOLT
!
REMEMBER, A CELEBRITY SHOULD ALWAYS WALK WITH A STRAIGHT BACK...
A-Are you...crying?
...
MOKO...
WHA?
?!
fwip

MOOOKOOOOOO!
RADIANT
!
I miiiissed yooooou!
WAAAH
WAAAH
...
S...

STOP RIGHT THEEEEERE!
FREEZE

Wha?
TMP
How could you... why did you stop me?
You could've stopped me with a touch, like always.
Bulldozing you does not count as "a touch"!
I COULDN'T HELP BUT STOP YOU...
...WHEN YOU RUSHED ME LOOKING LIKE THAT!

Huh?
Looking like what?
Was my expression so full of desire?
?
The way you look right now!
N-O!!
Huh?
This?
I recognize...
...that look...
I've seen it before.
Right after I saw that harmless expression, I experienced a terror that made my blood freeze...
Yes...
That was when you were plotting to force me to join the Love Me Section!
The Love Me Section is a great place to belong.
It's fun.
It's a real bargain.
A radiant saleswoman's sales smile
And the terror right after.
What...

...ARE YOU PLOTTING THIS TIME?!
What?!
I-I'm not plotting anything.
YOU'RE LYING!
YOU CAN'T FOOL ME!
YOU MUST BE HIDING SOMETHING FROM ME!
I...I'm not—
IF YOU WON'T TELL ME...
...I WON'T TALK TO YOU FOR A WHOLE YEAR!
CRUMBLE
Her saleswoman's smile

G...
LOOOOOOOM
.....
IS...
...THAT ALL?
THE REASON YOU'RE SO DOWN?
I COULD TELL JUST FROM LOOK-ING AT YOUR BACK THAT YOU WERE MAKING FACES LIKE THE WORLD WAS GONNA END.

SO YOU DON'T HAVE ANYTHING TO WEAR TO THE PARTY TONIGHT?
WHY LOOK SO HOPELESS ABOUT SOMETHING AS SIMPLE AS THAT?
I don't get it at all.
.....
IT'S GONNA BE...
...AN UNBELIEVABLY GORGEOUS PARTY...
DARK MOON HAS ATTRACTED A LOT OF ATTENTION. IT'S A LARGE-SCALE DRAMA.
THE AFTER-PARTY WAS ALWAYS GOING TO BE A BIG ONE...
...BUT THE RATINGS...
...FINALLY EXCEEDED TSUKIGOMORI TWO WEEKS AGO...
...SO THE PARTY IS GOING TO BE EVEN MORE GORGEOUS TO CELEBRATE THAT...

TV CREWS WILL BE THERE...
...AND THE ACTORS AND CREW WILL ALL BE GORGEOUSLY DRESSED TO MATCH THE VENUE...
...AND THE ATMOSPHERE WILL BE SOMETHING LIKE THE JAPAN ACADEMY AWARDS...
THAT'S PRETTY EXTRA-ORDI-NARY...
I THINK...
...I'M THE ONLY ONE...
...WHO'S ATTEMPTING TO WEAR...
What she plans to wear
Heh heh heh
...EVERYDAY CLOTHES TO A FANCY PLACE LIKE THAT...
WELL...
I WONDER IF I'LL ACTUALLY BE ABLE TO ATTEND...
I CAN IMAGINE...
...BE-ING...
...DENIED ENTRY CUZ NO ONE BELIEVES I'M AN ACTRESS...
I'M KYOKO, I PLAYED MIO!
DON'T LIE! YOU LOOK NOTHING LIKE HER!
Do you think I'm stupid?!
The guard
Enough already, or I'll call the police!
...

I-I SEE...
I CAN SEE WHY SHE'S SO DOWN...
WHY DON'T YOU BORROW SOMETHING FROM THE AGENCY?
You borrowed Natsu's costumes from the agency.
THEN...
...
UH...
WELL... UM...
I WORRY ABOUT ALWAYS DEPENDING ON THEM...
WHAT'RE YOU SAYING? THE AGENCY'S WARDROBE IS THERE FOR THE ACTORS AND TALENTOS.
You don't need to feel so bad.
AFTER-PARTIES ARE PART OF YOUR JOB...
...SO THE AGENCY WILL GLADLY LEND YOU SOMETHING.
...

YEAH...
YOU'RE...
...RIGHT...
THEN... I'LL...
...ASK... THE PRESIDENT THIS TIME TOO...
BOO
...
WHAT'S WRONG?
THIS ISN'T LIKE YOU.
YOU DON'T HATE THESE SORTS OF PARTIES.
MAYBE...
...YOU DON'T WANT TO ATTEND THE PARTY AT ALL?
Unlike me, who hates interacting needlessly with other people.
WHY'RE YOU SO RELUC-TANT?

N...
...O.
NO.
Why would I...
...feel that way?
RADIANT
NO WAY, NO WAY.
That's impossible.
I'VE BEEN REALLY LOOKING FORWARD TO IT.
Although I am nervous that my first after-party is such a gorgeous one.
Kyah ha!
...
--

chak
Ah!
I SHOULD GO SEE MR. SAWARA OR THE PRESIDENT!
SORRY, MOKO.
I HAVE TO GO CUZ I NEED TO GET READY.
rise
I'll tell you how the party goes.
Thanks for listening to me. ♡
Okay.
See you! ♡
kachak
.....
WHAT WAS THAT?
WHY'D SHE HAVE HER SALESWOMAN'S SMILE ON JUST THEN?
...

MAYBE...
...YOU DON'T WANT TO ATTEND THE PARTY AT ALL?
HUH?
WAS I...
...RIGHT?
WHAT?
...WHY?

DARN...
MY...
...THOUGHTS SHOWED THROUGH...
I'M A FAILURE AS AN ACTRESS...
WILL SHE...
...FIGURE OUT...
...THE REAL REASON...
...THAT...
...I DON'T WANT...
...TO ATTEND THE PARTY?

...
I...
...WASN'T WORRIED ABOUT WHAT TO WEAR...
WHEN I ASKED MR. SAWARA ABOUT IT...
...HE SAID MY SCHOOL UNIFORM WOULD BE ACCEPTABLE.
I CONSIDER MY UNIFORM...
...APPROPRIATE TO MY STATUS ANYWAY...
...SO I WAS RELIEVED...
...INSTEAD OF EMBARRASSED.
BUT...
I...
...COULDN'T THINK OF ANOTHER EXCUSE...
"I DON'T HAVE ANYTHING TO WEAR TO THE PARTY."
SO...
...I MADE THAT MY EXCUSE.

CUZ...
I...
...DON'T WANT...
...ANY-BODY...
...TO FIGURE OUT THE REAL REASON.
AH...
YOU'RE RIGHT.

IT'S...
...
REALLY
...
...GIVING
ME
COURAGE
...

THAT'S WHEN ...
I HEARD...
...AN UNPLEASANT SOUND.

DEEP...
...DEEP...
...REALLY DEEP...
...IN MY HEART...
WHERE I HAD PUT SO MANY, MANY LOCKS ON IT...
...THAT IT SHOULD HAVE NEVER OPENED AGAIN...
THE BOX THAT I...
...THOUGHT WAS FOREVER SEALED...
I HEARD...
...THE LAST LOCK CLICKING...

I'VE...
...EXPERI-ENCED...
...NOT SO LONG AGO...
...THE SAME KIND OF EMO-TION...
End of Act 170

Skip-Beat! End Notes

Everyone knows how to be a fan, but sometimes cool things from other cultures need a little help crossing the language barrier.

Page 5, panel 1: Yorozuya
Yorozuya means "a dealer in all sorts of articles," and tends to refer to a general store, but here it is the name of the store.

Page 13, panel 1: Initial █████
Refers to *Initial D,* a manga about street racing.

Page 125, panel 2: Ketchup on omelet rice
Writing things on omelet rice in ketchup is a common way to serve the dish. Some maid cafés even offer a service where the maid will draw or write things on your omelet rice.

Page 155, panel 6: "Win against the enemy"
The *teki* from *steki* (steak) can be read as "enemy" and the *katsu* (pork cutlet) can be read as "to win."

Yoshiki Nakamura is originally from Tokushima Prefecture. She started drawing manga in elementary school, which eventually led to her 1993 debut of *Yume de Au yori Suteki* (Better than Seeing in a Dream) in *Hana to Yume* magazine. Her other works include the basketball series *Saint Love*, *MVP wa Yuzurenai* (Can't Give Up MVP), *Blue Wars* and *Tokyo Crazy Paradise*, a series about a female bodyguard in 2020 Tokyo.

Shojo Beat

SKIP·BEAT!

Vol. 28

Shojo Beat Edition

STORY AND ART BY YOSHIKI NAKAMURA

English Translation & Adaptation/Tomo Kimura
Touch-up Art & Lettering/Sabrina Heep
Design/Ronnie Casson
Editor/Pancha Diaz

Printed in the U.S.A.

Published by VIZ Media, LLC
P.O. Box 77010
San Francisco, CA 94107

10 9 8 7 6 5 4 3 2 1
First printing, July 2012

PARENTAL ADVISORY
SKIP·BEAT! is rated T for Teen and is recommended for ages 13 and up. This volume contains a grudge.
ratings.viz.com

SURPRISE!

You may be reading the wrong way!

It's true: In keeping with the original Japanese comic format, this book reads from right to left—so action, sound effects, and word balloons are completely reversed. This preserves the orientation of the original artwork—plus, it's fun! Check out the diagram shown here to get the hang of things, and then turn to the other side of the book to get started!

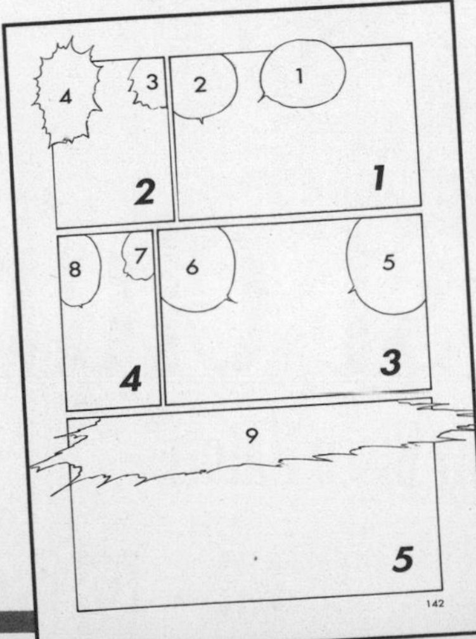